REPORT

Deregulating School Aid in California

Revenues and Expenditures in the Second Year of Categorical Flexibility

Jennifer Imazeki

Supported by the William and Flora Hewlett Foundation, the Dirk and Charlene Kabcenell Foundation, and the Stuart Foundation

RAND EDUCATION

**Policy
Analysis for
California
Education**

PACE

www.edpolicyinca.org

The research described in this report was supported by the William and Flora Hewlett Foundation, the Dirk and Charlene Kabcenell Foundation, and the Stuart Foundation, and was conducted by PACE research network and RAND Education, a division of the RAND Corporation.

Library of Congress Control Number: 2012941293

ISBN: 978-0-8330-7520-8

Published 2012 by the RAND Corporation
1776 Main Street, P.O. Box 2138, Santa Monica, CA 90407-2138
1200 South Hayes Street, Arlington, VA 22202-5050
4570 Fifth Avenue, Suite 600, Pittsburgh, PA 15213-2665
RAND URL: http://www.rand.org/
To order RAND documents or to obtain additional information, contact
Distribution Services: Telephone: (310) 451-7002;
Fax: (310) 451-6915; Email: order@rand.org

Preface

In 2010, researchers at the RAND Corporation, the University of California at Berkeley and Davis, and San Diego State University joined together to study the impact of a new state policy that increased flexibility over a large number of previously restricted categorical programs. The objective of the project overall is to gather evidence about how districts have responded to the fiscal freedom, particularly how resource allocations are made at the district level and what specific changes districts have made in their allocations. This report focuses on statewide data and describes statewide patterns in district revenues and expenditures since categorical flexibility went into effect.

Other reports from this project entitled "Deregulating School Aid in California" include

- J. Imazeki, *Deregulation of School Aid in California: Revenues and Expenditures in the First Year of Categorical Flexibility*, 2011.
- B. Fuller, J. Marsh, B. Stecher, and T. Timar, *Deregulating School Aid in California: How 10 Districts Responded to Fiscal Flexibility, 2009–2010*, 2011.
- B. M. Stecher, B. Fuller, T. Timar, and J. A. Marsh, *Deregulating School Aid in California: How Districts Responded to Flexibility in Tier 3 Categorical Funds in 2010–2011*, 2012.

Funding to support this research has been provided by The William and Flora Hewlett Foundation, the Dirk and Charlene Kabcenell Foundation, and the Stuart Foundation. This report should be of interest to policymakers, education researchers, and other stakeholders in the education community.

Contents

Figure and Tables

Figure

Tables

Summary

For decades, policymakers and researchers have been debating the effectiveness of California's highly regulated and prescriptive system of school finance. For much of that time, a chief target of critics has been the large share of funding that is allocated through categorical programs, that is, programs where funding is contingent upon districts using the money in a particular way or for a particular purpose. In 2007–08, roughly two-fifths of state[1] school spending on K–12 education was allocated via more than 60 separate programs, each with its own set of restrictions on how the funds from that program could be spent. In 2008–09, the strings were taken off 40 of those programs, collectively known as the "Tier 3" programs, as part of a budget deal that also reduced the funding for those programs.[2]

In 2010, researchers at the RAND Corporation, the University of California at Berkeley and Davis, and San Diego State University joined together to study the impact of the new policy. The objective of the research is to gather evidence about how districts have responded to the fiscal freedom, particularly how resource allocations are made at the district level and what specific changes districts have made in their allocations. Understanding how districts have responded to the Tier 3 flexibility is particularly important in light of Governor Jerry Brown's recent proposal to largely dismantle the remaining categorical programs and move to a weighted school finance formula that would dramatically increase the control that districts have to spend their budgets as they wish.

The project's overall research questions were the following:

1. What did district leaders do with the newly flexible Tier 3 funds?
2. How did district leaders make these allocation decisions, and who was involved?
3. What were the reported local consequences of these allocation decisions?
4. What prior conditions and concurrent factors shaped budget decision of district leaders?
5. How did federal Title I stimulus funds interact with decisions about Tier 3 flexibility?
6. What are statewide revenue and spending patterns for Tier 3 and stimulus funds?
   a. Which kinds of districts, schools, and students benefit most from the flow of deregulated Tier 3 categorical aid and federal stimulus dollars?

---

[1] This refers to revenue only from the state general fund and other state sources and does not include federal or local funds. That is, of the money allocated to districts from the state, about 40 percent was disbursed through categorical programs.

[2] See Fuller et al. (2011) for a full discussion of the history of California's categoricals and the passage of the Tier 3 flexibility legislation.

b. Do districts (and schools) with larger shares of Tier 3 and federal stimulus funding (as fractions of their overall budgets) spend relatively more or less on instruction and teaching staff, compared with districts that receive less from these sources?

The first five questions are addressed through in-depth case studies of ten districts, detailed in Fuller et al. (2011), and a statewide survey of district administrators, discussed in Stecher et al. (2012). Imazeki (2011) provided preliminary answers to the sixth question using comprehensive accounting and administrative data for all districts.

This report supports and extends the analysis in Imazeki (2011) in three ways. First, the previous report discussed revenues and spending patterns in the 2007–08 and 2008–09 school years; the analysis here adds data from 2009–10, the first full year of Tier 3 flexibility. Second, this report provides technical details about the data and variables that were not included in the earlier policy-oriented brief. Finally, this report presents as much of the data as possible, summarizing multiple measures of revenues and expenditures by district characteristics and exploring the patterns across districts.

Data

All the financial data for this analysis come from the California Department of Education's Standardized Account Code Structure (SACS) files. Data on district revenues and expenditures are combined with district characteristics, including district type (elementary, high school, or unified), fiscal health, Basic Aid status,[3] urban category, size, student performance (measured with the Academic Performance Index), percentage of students in poverty, and percentage of English learners. Revenue per pupil from the flexed Tier 3 programs, as well as federal stimulus funds and all restricted revenue, is compared to total revenue per pupil. In the analysis of expenditures, spending is broken into seven categories based on what items are purchased (instructional personnel, instruction materials, instruction-related personnel, other instruction-related materials, pupil services, local education agency [LEA] administration, and all other) and into eight categories based on educational goals (pre-K, general K–12, alternative education, adult education, supplemental education, special education, other instructional or service goals, and goals unrelated to instruction services).

Although the SACS system provides detailed information on the source and use of district monies, there are several limitations as well. Aside from the lag in availability that restricts this analysis to the years through 2009–10, a particular problem is that Tier 3 funds (and associated spending) cannot be identified after the 2008–09 school year. Therefore, only broad conclusions can be drawn about changes in district spending, based on changes in total expenditures.

---

[3] Districts with Basic Aid status are those districts with local property tax revenue above their state-determined revenue limit. Because districts can keep the excess tax revenue, Basic Aid districts typically have more unrestricted funds and higher revenue overall.

Findings

Districts receiving the highest levels of Tier 3 revenue per pupil, and with the largest budget shares coming from Tier 3 programs, tend to be high school districts and large districts in urban areas, serving larger proportions of high-need students (i.e., low-performing, in poverty, English learners). Given that funding for Tier 3 programs was reduced at the same time that more flexibility was granted, concerns have been raised that these districts with relatively more Tier 3 funding have been disproportionately affected by the state's budget crisis. However, the data show that districts with more Tier 3 funding lost a similar share of their budget as did other districts (although that represents larger per-pupil dollar amounts). Furthermore, so far and on average, districts do not appear to be making large-scale changes in how they are spending their money. As budgets have shrunk, districts are clearly trying to protect core programs, particularly instructional personnel and special education programs. There is a great deal of variation in how districts have responded to the budget cuts and to Tier 3 flexibility, but that variation does not seem to be strongly correlated with any observable district characteristics. These observations might be some comfort to those who have feared that higher-need districts would be disproportionately affected or that districts would simply abandon programs for higher-need students without the requirements of the categorical program regulations. On the other hand, districts with comparatively more Tier 3 revenue per pupil do seem to have made relatively larger cuts in programs for alternative and adult education, so the impact on students in these programs is unclear.

Several important caveats need to be considered. The analysis here is fairly broad in scope and only considers data through the first year after the policy went into effect, so districts had relatively little opportunity to make any major changes. In addition, it was (and still is) unclear whether the flexibility will last beyond the legislated sunset date in 2014; thus, some districts may have been reluctant to make major changes anyway. Perhaps most important, it is nearly impossible to separate the effect of increased flexibility from the overall reduction in resources experienced by almost all districts in the past few years. The two undoubtedly interacted as many districts used the additional freedom over Tier 3 funds to compensate for reductions in general funding levels. To the extent that districts made changes in their spending patterns, there is no way to determine whether similar changes would have been made without the accompanying budget cuts.

Acknowledgments

The research described in this report was sponsored by the William and Flora Hewlett Foundation, the Dirk and Charlene Kabcenell Foundation, and the Stuart Foundation. Lawrence Picus and Gema Zamarro reviewed the document and offered helpful suggestions that improved the final report. Donna White helped to prepare the document.

Abbreviations

ADA   average daily attendance
API   Academic Performance Index
CBEDS   California Basic Educational Data System
CDE   California Department of Education
EL   English learner
GATE   gifted and talented education
LAUSD   Los Angeles Unified School District
LEA   local education agency
PACE   Policy Analysis for California Education
PAIF   Professional Assignment Information Form
SACS   Standard Account Code Structure
SFSF   State Fiscal Stabilization Fund

CHAPTER ONE

Introduction

For decades, policymakers and researchers have been debating the effectiveness of California's highly regulated and prescriptive system of school finance. For much of that time, a chief target of critics has been the large share of funding that is allocated through categorical programs; that is, programs whose funding is contingent on districts using the money in a particular way or for a particular purpose. In 2007–08, roughly two-fifths of the state's school spending[1] on K–12 education was allocated via more than 60 separate programs, each with its own set of restrictions on how the funds from that program could be spent. In 2008–09, the strings were taken off 40 of those programs, collectively known as the "Tier 3" programs, as part of a budget deal that also reduced the funding for those programs.[2]

The new flexibility over the funds for the Tier 3 programs provides an opportunity to empirically assess at least some of the arguments that have been made for and against categorical funding. On the one hand, supporters of categorical programs have expressed concern that without the specific requirements imposed by the regulations, districts will not provide sufficient assistance for high-need students. On the other hand, critics have argued that local stakeholders should have more of a role in determining the priorities for individual districts, a role that categorical programs inherently take away (see Legislative Analyst, 1993; and Timar, 2007, for a review of the arguments for and against categorical program reform). This debate has taken on new urgency with Governor Jerry Brown's proposal to replace the current, overly complex and irrational system of school finance with a weighted funding formula that would give districts substantially more freedom over how they spend their budgets.[3]

To date, there is little empirical evidence about how districts in California might respond to widespread deregulation. Although there have been periodic attempts to consolidate some categorical programs, no prior reforms have involved as many programs or as large a share of districts' budgets as Tier 3 flexibility.

In 2010, researchers at the RAND Corporation, the University of California at Berkeley and Davis, and San Diego State University joined together to study the impact of the new policy. Our objective is to gather evidence about how districts have responded to the fiscal

---

[1] This refers to revenue only from the state general fund and other state sources and does not include federal or local funds. That is, of the money allocated to districts from the state, about 40 percent was disbursed through categorical programs.

[2] See Fuller et al. (2011) for a full discussion of the history of California's categoricals and the passage of the Tier 3 flexibility legislation.

[3] The weighted funding formula would essentially get rid of all categorical programs, with their accompanying requirements, and allocate money based on a formula where districts receive an equal amount for every student, with additional funding for certain high-need students. See Imazeki (2007) for a full discussion of the advantages and disadvantages of such a system.

freedom, particularly how resource allocations are made at the district level and what specific changes districts have made in their allocations. The project's overall research questions include the following:

1. What did district leaders do with the newly flexible Tier 3 funds?
2. How did district leaders make these allocation decisions, and who was involved?
3. What were the reported local consequences of these allocation decisions?
4. What prior conditions and concurrent factors shaped budget decision of district leaders?
5. How did federal Title I stimulus funds interact with decisions about Tier 3 flexibility?
6. What are statewide revenue and spending patterns for Tier 3 and stimulus funds?
    a. Which kinds of districts, schools, and students benefit most from the flow of deregulated Tier 3 categorical aid and federal stimulus dollars?
    a. Do districts (and schools) with larger shares of Tier 3 and federal stimulus funding (as fractions of their overall budgets) spend relatively more or less on instruction and teaching staff, compared with districts that benefit less from these sources?

The first five questions are addressed through in-depth case studies of ten districts, detailed in Fuller et al. (2011), and a statewide survey of district administrators, discussed in Stecher et al. (2012). An earlier policy brief (Imazeki, 2011) provided preliminary answers to the sixth question using comprehensive accounting and administrative data for all districts.

This report supports and extends the analysis in Imazeki (2011) in three ways. First, the previous report discussed revenues and spending patterns in the 2007–08 and 2008–09 school years; the analysis here adds data from 2009–10, the first full year of Tier 3 flexibility. Second, this report provides technical details about the data and variables that were not included in the earlier policy-oriented brief. Finally, this report presents as much of the data itself as possible, summarizing multiple measures of revenues and expenditures by district characteristics and exploring the patterns across districts.

The specific research questions include the following:

*   **Revenue Levels.** How much total and per-pupil revenue do districts receive through Tier 3 and federal stimulus programs? How have these levels changed over time?
*   **Distribution of Revenue Levels.** Which districts have received the most Tier 3 and stimulus dollars per pupil? Are there identifiable patterns based on district characteristics (district type, fiscal health, Basic Aid status, level of urbanicity, and enrollment) or student characteristics (such as student performance, income, and English learner [EL] status)?
*   **Distribution of Revenue Shares.** Which districts have the most Tier 3 and other restricted revenue as a share of all revenues? Are there identifiable patterns based on district or student characteristics?
*   **Distribution of Revenue Changes**. Which districts have experienced the largest changes in Tier 3 and overall revenue per pupil (in dollars per pupil and as a percentage of all revenue)? Are there identifiable patterns based on district or student characteristics?
*   **Spending Priorities**. How do districts spend Tier 3 dollars? How do they spend total overall revenue?

- **Spending Distribution.** Do districts with larger shares of Tier 3 funding have different spending patterns, particularly for instruction and teaching staff, compared to those with less Tier 3 funding?

To answer these questions, I use data from the California Department of Education's Standardized Account Code Structure (SACS) files, which provide detailed information on the source and use of district monies. Chapter Three provides a full explanation of how the data are organized, as well as a thorough discussion of some important limitations of the data. Before that, Chapter Two provides background information on the policy that granted the Tier 3 flexibility and examines revenue levels for the state as a whole in 2007–08, 2008–09, and 2009–10. Chapter Four explores how revenues per pupil are distributed across districts, and Chapter Five examines patterns in district spending. The final chapter summarizes all the empirical findings and discusses them within the current policy context, reiterating some important caveats.

CHAPTER TWO

Background

California school districts receive the largest share of their funding (roughly 80 percent) from the state. This state funding is allocated either through revenue limits, which are unrestricted general funds, or categorical programs, which require that the funds be spent for the specific purpose designated by the program. Most districts also receive funding from the federal government, most of which is restricted similarly to state categorical funds; the largest federal programs include Title I, for students in poverty, and the Individuals with Disability Education Act (IDEA) for students with disabilities. Local funds make up a very small share (about 6.5 percent) of district budgets.

Categorical flexibility was adopted as part of the 2007–08 budget deal. In that legislation, all categorical programs were assigned to one of three tiers (see Tables 2.1 and 2.2). Tier 1 programs were left largely intact; funding was not cut, but neither was any flexibility granted.[1] No flexibility was granted for Tier 2 programs either, but they experienced some reductions in funding. Tier 3 programs saw the biggest cuts, and districts were given complete flexibility to use the funds for any educational purpose. The original legislation extended flexibility until 2013[2] and froze each district's annual Tier 3 allocation at its 2008–09 proportional share. That is, if a district received 1 percent of total program funding in 2008–09, it will receive 1 percent of total program funding in each the following years. Thus, the actual dollar amount each district receives for Tier 3 programs will only change if the total state appropriations for the Tier 3 programs change.

It is important to point out that categorical flexibility, and the corresponding cuts in funding, went into effect at the same time that districts began receiving funds from the federal government's stimulus package, the American Recovery and Reinvestment Act of 2009. Stimulus funds were allocated in 2008–09 and 2009–10; districts could carry over funds to 2010–11, but funds were supposed to be entirely spent by September 2011. The way some of the stimulus funds were allocated was directly tied to reductions in state revenues; for example, appropriations from the State Fiscal Stabilization Fund (SFSF) were directly correlated with reductions in certain categorical funding.

Figure 2.1 shows total revenue for districts from all sources.[3] Between federal and state categorical programs (including Tier 3), 31 percent ($16.6 billion) of districts' total revenue in

---

[1] Tier 1 does include K–3 class size reduction. Some of those regulations were loosened, but the appropriation was not reduced.

[2] The sunset date has been extended to the end of the 2014–15 school year.

[3] The totals here are only for districts with complete data and do not include county offices. See Chapter Three for a full explanation of the data used.

Table 2.1
Categorical Programs in Tiers 1 and 2

Program	2010–11 Funding ($ millions)
Tier 1	
Special Education	3,107
Economic Impact Aid	942
K–3 Class Size Reduction	935
After School Education and Safety	547
Home-to-School Transportation	496
Quality Education Investment Act	402
Child nutrition	151
Tier 2	
Student assessments	71
Charter school facility grants	61
Year-round school grants	31
Partnership Academies	19
Apprentice programs	16
Foster youth programs	15
Adults in correctional facilities	15
County office oversight	9
K–12 High-Speed Network	8
Agricultural vocational education	4
Total	**6,830**

Table 2.2
Categorical Programs in Tier 3

Program	2010–11 Funding ($ millions)
Targeted Instructional Improvement Block Grant	855
Adult education	635
Regional Occupational Centers and Programs	385
School and Library Improvement Block Grant	370
Supplemental instruction	336
Instructional Materials Block Grant	334
Deferred maintenance	251
Professional Development Block Grant	218
Grade 7–12 counseling	167
Charter Schools Categorical Block Grant	142
Teacher Credentialing Block Grant	90
Arts and Music Block Grant	88
School Safety Block Grant	80
Ninth-Grade Class Size Reduction	79
Pupil Retention Block Grant	77
California High School Exit Exam supplemental instruction	58

Table 2.2—Continued

Program	2010–11 Funding ($ millions)
California School Age Families Education	46
Professional Development Institutes for Math and English	45
Gifted and Talented Education	44
Community Day Schools	42
Community Based English Tutoring	40
Physical Education Block Grant	34
Alternative Credentialing/Internship programs	26
Peer Assistance and Review	24
School Safety Competitive Grants	14
California Technology Assistance Projects	14
Certificated Staff Mentoring	9
County offices of education Williams audits[a]	8
Specialized Secondary Programs	5
Principal Training	4
American Indian Education Centers	4
Oral health assessments	4
Advanced Placement fee waivers	2
National Board certification incentive grants	2
Bilingual teacher training assistance program	2
American Indian Early Education Program	1
Reader services for blind teachers	—[b]
Center for Civic Education	—[b]
Teacher dismissal apportionments	—[b]
California Association of Student Councils	—[b]
Total	**4,537**

[a]Williams audits are required to ensure compliance with the Williams court case, in which the state agreed to provide all students equal access to instructional materials, safe schools, and quality teachers.

[b]Statewide, less than $500,000 is spent on each of these programs.

2007–08 was restricted in some way. Tier 3 categorical programs accounted for just over $4.5 billion of that, equivalent to 8.4 percent of total district revenue, or 27 percent of all restricted revenue.

When flexibility was granted for the Tier 3 programs, their funding was also reduced, so Tier 3 revenue fell in 2008–09, to $3.4 billion. However, *total* district revenue actually went up slightly, because federal stimulus funding filled in for the drop in state funds. The bulk of stimulus funds was allocated in 2008–09; once those funds were spent, 2009–10 revenue dropped significantly (10 percent overall).[4] Restricted revenue in 2009–10 from all sources

---

4 Districts were allowed to spread out the spending of stimulus funds through 2010–11, but the funds were appropriated in 2008–09 and 2009–10; therefore, I include them with revenues for those years.

Figure 2.1
Total Revenues, 2007–09 to 2009–10

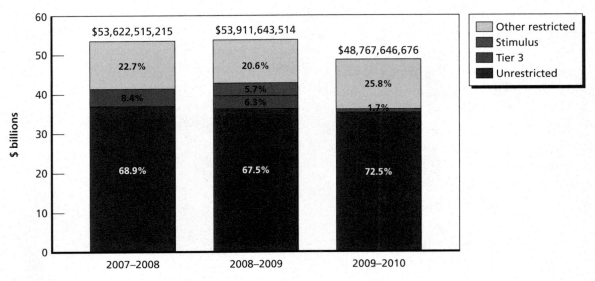

($13.4 billion) fell more than unrestricted revenue ($35.3 billion) and Tier 3 funding became unrestricted.[5] Thus, although there was less money overall, districts had greater control over a larger *share* (72.5 percent) of their budgets. As will be discussed in Chapter Four, districts varied greatly in the percentage of revenue that was restricted, and there was correspondingly large variation in how much the restricted share increased after Tier 3 flexibility went into effect.

---

[5] Districts still received allocations specifically for Tier 3 programs; however, the money was treated as unrestricted and, in the accounting data used here, it is not possible to identify those revenues separately from other unrestricted revenue in 2009–10. Thus, in Figure 2.1, Tier 3 monies are simply included with unrestricted revenue.

CHAPTER THREE

Data

All the financial data for this analysis come from the California Department of Education's SACS files. The SACS system uses different types of codes to provide extremely detailed information on the source and use of district monies. The four code types used to categorize the data in this report are Resource, Function, Object, and Goal. *Resource codes* are used primarily with revenues and identify the source of dollars when there are restrictions on how the funds are spent. For example, resource code 3010 identifies funds from Title I, Part A, Basic Grants, and code 3012 is for funds from Title I, Part A, Program Improvement School Assistance and Intervention Teams. *Function codes* are used primarily with expenditures; they identify the purpose for which dollars are spent, such as instruction or administration. *Object codes* can be used with either revenues or expenditures; only the expenditure objects are used here and they identify the items bought, such as salaries or books.[1] *Goal codes* identify the general objective or instructional setting, such as general education or adult education.[2]

By restricting our attention to certain codes or combinations of codes, we can use the SACS data to isolate revenues and expenditures at an extremely fine level of detail. For example, it is possible to identify how much of the revenue from a particular resource was spent on instructional salaries for general education versus instruction-related materials for special education. One drawback of the SACS is the lag in availability; because the files are released in the spring following a fiscal year, data for 2010–11 are not available until spring 2012. Thus, the analysis here only uses data through 2009–10.

Revenue Data

I use resource codes to divide revenues into unrestricted and restricted sources (see Figure 2.1). Prior to 2009–10, each categorical program had its own resource code. Consequently, for 2007–08 and 2008–09, it is possible to determine exactly how much revenue districts received from each program in the Tier 3 group. The budget legislation that created Tier 3 flexibility said that districts were free from program or funding requirements. The California Department of Education (CDE) interpreted this to mean that those funds should be considered

---

[1] Revenue objects identify the general source and type of funds, such as local taxes or federal funds that may be used for more than one program. Revenue objects can be used in conjunction with resource codes to identify the source (state, federal, local) when the funds are unrestricted.

[2] Revenues and expenditures here are also restricted to Funds 1 (General Fund), 11 (Adult Education), and 12 (Child Development Fund). For a full explanation of the SACS codes, see the *California School Accounting Manual* (California Department of Education, 2011b).

unrestricted, so the CDE discontinued use of the restricted resource codes beginning with the 2009–10 SACS.[3] Unfortunately, this means that Tier 3 monies (revenue or expenditures) cannot be identified in the SACS after 2008–09. In addition, because Tier 3 flexibility officially went into effect halfway through the 2008–09 fiscal year, districts were given the option to discontinue use of the resource codes immediately. Although most districts did not change their accounting procedures until the following year, some did, and that will create additional "noise" in the 2008–09 SACS data when trying to identify Tier 3 funds.

To identify the source of district revenues, one alternative to the SACS is the apportionment (or appropriations) files that are available from the CDE. Those files have the advantage of being available sooner (certified data for 2010–11 were available in June 2011) and contain the apportionments for the Tier 3 programs. See Weston (2011) for a detailed analysis of the Tier 3 programs using those data. However, while the apportionment data are more useful for analysis of revenues, they cannot provide any information about how districts use those funds, which is one of the key areas of interest here. For consistency, I use the SACS data for both revenues and expenditures.

The one category of revenues for which I use apportionment files instead of the SACS is federal stimulus revenue (from the American Recovery and Reinvestment Act) in 2008–09 and 2009–10. Because of apparent confusion over the amount, timing, and restrictions on stimulus funds, there is a significant amount of error in the SACS data with regard to the stimulus funds, and the apportionment files are considerably more reliable. For the purposes of this report, "stimulus funding" is restricted to stimulus funds allocated through Title IA program and the SFSF. The legislature specifically used money from the SFSF to offset cuts in revenue limit funding and in certain categorical programs.

Expenditures

In the analysis of expenditures, I divide expenditures in two ways. One set of categories is based on combinations of function and object codes; the other relies on goal codes. The six function-object categories are listed in Table 3.1.

Table 3.1
Function-Object Categories

Category	Codes
Instructional salaries and benefits	Functions: 1000–1999 Objects: 1000–3999
Other instruction (books and materials, services)	Functions: 1000–1999 Objects: 4000–7499
Instruction-related salaries and benefits (supervision and administration, library, media and technology, school administration)	Functions: 2000–2999 Objects: 4000–7499
Pupil services (counseling, food services, transportation)	Functions: 3000–3999 All Objects
Local education agency (LEA) administration	Functions: 7000–7999 All Objects
All other (ancillary services, community services, enterprise, plant services)	Functions: 4000–6999 All Objects

---

[3] See CDE memo, 2009.

The eight goal categories are listed in Table 3.2.

It is worth noting that since the flexibility provisions were adopted, the California Department of Education has compiled an annual report on total expenditures broken down by goal and some function codes (see CDE, 2011a). Data files accompanying that report provide the specific expenditures in each individual district.

Table 3.2
Goal Categories

Category	Codes
Undistributed (not related to instruction or services)	0000
Pre-K	0001–0999
General K–12	1000–1999
Alternative education	3100–3800
Adult education	4000–4749
Supplemental education	4750–4999
Special education	5000–5999
Other goals (nonagency, services)	6000–9999

Limitations of SACS Data

Perhaps the biggest question that policymakers and education stakeholders have about Tier 3 flexibility is whether removing the specific requirements led districts to stop offering the intended services. However, a huge complicating factor in identifying the causal effect of flexibility alone is that the policy change went into effect at the same time as large budget cuts that left most districts struggling simply to maintain core services. Districts did receive federal stimulus money in 2008 and 2009 to offset some of these budget cuts, but certainly one expectation at the time was that districts would use their new budgetary freedom over Tier 3 dollars to offset at least some of the cuts in their general funds.

The case studies in Fuller et al. (2011) suggest that there has been a wide range of responses to the policy change. Some districts "swept" all their Tier 3 funds into the general fund and cut programs entirely; others worked hard to maintain Tier 3 programs, even if at reduced levels. Unfortunately, although the SACS allows for a relatively fine level of detail about expenditures, items are not generally coded in a way that allows for the identification of specific programs, like gifted and talented education (GATE) or extra help for students who fail the high school exit exam. In the past, SACS *revenue* codes could be used to identify the spending on these programs, since the categorical requirements meant that funds coming from a certain program (like GATE) must be spent on that program. Without the revenue codes for the specific program funds, there is no longer any way to identify expenditures on those specific programs.[4]

What the SACS expenditures codes can identify is the general goal and function for which monies are spent. For example, although I can no longer identify exactly how much

---

[4] Some of those programmatic changes might be identified with the Professional Assignment Information Form (PAIF) files, collected as part of the California Basic Educational Data System (CBEDS). However, staff assignment information (indicating exactly what subject a teacher was assigned to teach) was not collected in 2009–10.

is spent on tutoring for the California High School Exit Examination (CAHSEE), there is a goal code for all spending on "supplemental education." However, that would also include expenditures for all other programs that assist students with extra needs. Thus, although the analysis here is consistent with the finding in Fuller et al. (2011) that districts were reducing or eliminating certain Tier 3 programs, in most cases, I cannot pinpoint specific programs. One exception is Adult Education, which has its own goal code. It is also possible to see the extent to which districts protected teachers and instruction relative to other priorities.

Finally, this analysis only uses data for districts that have complete data for all three school years (2007–08, 2008–09, and 2009–10). Therefore, a dozen districts are dropped because of reorganizations, closures, and consolidations. I also dropped several districts with missing or questionable data (e.g., revenues twice as high in 2009–10 as in previous years). The final data set has 921 districts with complete data.

District Characteristics

The SACS data are combined with descriptive data about districts from the CDE. The district characteristics used are district type (elementary, high school, or unified), fiscal health, Basic Aid status, urban category, and size. Following Perry et al. (2007), the measure of fiscal health is an index that takes into account AB 1200 certification status,[5] deficit spending relative to reserves,[6] and actual reserves relative to required reserves.[7] An "Unhealthy" district either has had at least one "Negative" AB 1200 certification in the last three years or was in the bottom 30 percent of all districts for deficit spending relative to reserves (averaged over three years), or was in the bottom 30 percent of all districts for actual reserves relative to required reserves (average over three years). A "Healthy" district has only Positive certifications for the last three years *and* was in the top 70 percent of districts for deficit spending relative to reserves *and* was in the top 70 percent of districts for actual reserves relative to required reserves. All other districts are labeled "Marginal."

Districts with Basic Aid status are those districts with local property tax revenue above their state-determined revenue limit. Because districts can keep the excess tax revenue, Basic Aid districts typically have more unrestricted funds and higher revenue overall. There are seven urban categories, based on census definitions: large city, small and mid-size cities, large suburb, small and mid-size suburbs, town, metro rural and remote, nonmetro rural. Enrollment is based on average daily attendance (ADA).[8]

Districts are also described by the characteristics of their students, including student performance, measured with the district-level Academic Performance Index (API); percentage of students from poor families, measured by the share of students who are eligible for the federal Free or Reduced-Price Lunch Program; and percentage of English learners.

---

[5]   Under AB 1200, districts are required to submit two reports each year that indicate whether the district is able to meet its financial obligations. A "Negative" certification means that a district is unable to meet its financial obligations for the remainder of the current year or for the subsequent fiscal year."

[6]   Total revenues – total expenditures/total reserves.

[7]   Actual reserves – required reserves/average daily attendance (ADA).

[8]   Note that throughout the report, "per pupil" is used interchangeably with "per ADA."

The discussions of revenues and expenditures in Chapters Four and Five primarily highlight notable patterns with respect to these district characteristics, although tables with the full results for all variables are included.

Student-Weighted Means

In order to analyze how revenues and expenditures are distributed across continuous district characteristics, such as API and percentage in poverty, districts are grouped into quintiles, so that each group contains 20 percent of the districts. Given the wide range of district sizes, each quintile grouping may represent very different numbers of students. An alternative approach would be to weight the quintile cutoffs by ADA so that each quintile would contain 20 percent of the *students* in the state (and different numbers of districts). However, because the variables are all measured at the district level, not the student level, it seems more appropriate to use unweighted quintiles.[9]

Although the quintiles represent roughly equal numbers of districts, the averages within each quintile (and for all state-level averages) are weighted by the number of students throughout the analysis here. It is relatively common for averages of district per-pupil revenues and expenditures to be student-weighted (see, for example, Loeb, Grissom, and Strunk, 2007). District averages that are weighted by the number of pupils (or in this case, ADA) are then interpreted as representing the revenue or spending experienced by the average student within the averaged group of districts. One important reason to use student-weighted averages, particularly in California, is to reduce the weight given to very small districts, which typically are outliers with very high per-pupil revenues or spending simply because they have so few pupils by which to divide.

However, the huge range of district size in California also poses a problem for student-weighted averages. Specifically, with an ADA of roughly 550,000, the Los Angeles Unified School District (LAUSD) is several times larger than the next largest district (San Diego Unified, at around 106,000). With student-weighted averages, particularly for smaller subgroups of districts such as the quintiles, LAUSD swamps all other districts in its group.[10] In the analysis here, the inclusion or exclusion of Los Angeles generally does not have a substantial impact on the overall distributional patterns, but in a few cases, the pattern does look quite different.

Thus, if student weights are not used, small districts have a disproportionately large impact on their related averages, but if student weights are used, then LAUSD has a disproportionately large impact on its related averages. My solution here is to use student-weighted averages throughout but present the results both with and without Los Angeles. Note that only the categories that include Los Angeles are affected (e.g., Unified; Large City; the highest

---

[9] That is, with student-weighted quintiles, the highest poverty quintile would *not* represent the poorest 20 percent of students; it would represent the students in the *districts* with the highest percentage of students in poverty. Given that the variables are district-level variables, it seems more appropriate simply to use district-based quintiles.

[10] Another reason not to use student-weighted quintiles is that if student-weighted quintiles exacerbates this problem, whichever quintile contains LAUSD will have significantly fewer districts and Los Angeles will dominate the group even more.

quintiles of size, poverty, and Tier 3 revenue; fourth quintile of percentage of English Learners; and lowest quintile of API performance), so only those categories have two sets of averages reported in all the tables.

CHAPTER FOUR

Distribution of Revenue

Chapter Two detailed the level and changes in total revenue for all districts in the state. This chapter describes how Tier 3[1] and total district revenue per pupil are distributed across districts. Although districts with more Tier 3 revenue per pupil presumably benefit more from gaining additional flexibility, those programs also experienced deeper funding cuts, so it is worth investigating which districts were most affected.

Specifically, the key questions of interest are as follows:

- Which districts have received the most Tier 3 and stimulus dollars per pupil? Are there identifiable patterns based on district characteristics (district type, fiscal health, Basic Aid status, level of urbanicity and enrollment) or student characteristics (student performance, income, EL status)?
- Which districts have the most Tier 3 and other restricted revenue as a share of all revenues? Are there identifiable patterns based on district or student characteristics?
- Which districts have experienced the largest changes in Tier 3 and overall revenue per pupil (in dollars per pupil and as a percentage of all revenue)? Are there identifiable patterns based on district or student characteristics?

Revenue Levels

Total revenue per pupil, Tier 3 revenue per pupil, and stimulus revenue per pupil all vary widely across districts, as shown by the simple summary statistics in Table 4.1. As with total revenue for the state (shown in Figure 2.1), average pupil-weighted revenue per pupil went up slightly from 2007–08 to 2008–09 and then dropped in 2009–10. Average weighted Tier 3 revenue per pupil fell from 2007–08 to 2008–09, reflecting the cuts in those programs. It should be noted that Tier 3 levels in 2008–09 may be misleadingly low here because districts had the option of changing how they recorded Tier 3 monies mid-year; the majority of districts continued to code Tier 3 revenues as they had in previous years, but at least some districts chose to stop tracking Tier 3 funds immediately (so their totals in SACS will appear to be lower). Data from appropriations files suggest the revenue drop in 2008–09 was smaller than observed in the SACS (see Weston, 2011).

Table 4.2 shows weighted average revenues per pupil by district characteristics, and Table 4.3 shows weighted average revenues per pupil by district-level student characteristics.

---

[1] Tier 3 dollars cannot be identified in the SACS after 2008–09.

Table 4.1
ADA-Weighted Revenues per ADA, California School Districts, 2007–08 to 2009–10

	All Revenue per ADA 07–08	All Revenue per ADA 08–09	All Revenue per ADA 09–10	Tier 3 Revenue per ADA 07–08	Tier 3 Revenue per ADA 08–09	Stimulus Revenue per ADA 08–09	Stimulus Revenue per ADA 09–10
Revenues per ADA							
Mean	$10,052	$10,153	$9,308	$844	$684	$578	$157
Standard deviation	$1,696	$1,739	$1,833	$511	$476	$190	$96
Minimum	$6,955	$7,185	$6,261	$157	$14	$0	$0
Maximum	$49,025	$41,113	$46,586	$5,521	$4,159	$11,218	$1,045
Number of districts	921	921	921	921	867	921	921

Districts receiving relatively more Tier 3 revenue per pupil include high school districts, large urban districts, districts with lower-performing and higher-poverty students, and districts with more English Learners.[2] These patterns are largely consistent with the fact that many Tier 3 programs were targeted to these students. For example, Supplemental Instruction for the California High School Exit Exam and Ninth-Grade Class Size Reduction were allocated to high schools, whereas the Pupil Retention Block Grant and Supplemental Instruction programs were intended for districts with higher-need students. Because Los Angeles receives relatively high levels of Tier 3 revenue per pupil, the averages without LAUSD are all noticeably lower but the general patterns still hold.

There appears to be a substantial amount of overlap between districts receiving more Tier 3 revenue and those receiving more stimulus funding. This is not particularly surprising, given that stimulus funding included here is funding allocated for Title IA programs and the State Fiscal Stabilization Fund, which was used partly to offset cuts in categoricals.

The correlation between Tier 3 and stimulus funds is clearest in Table 4.4, which shows weighted average revenues per pupil by quintiles of Tier 3 revenue per pupil and the share of all revenue coming from Tier 3. Table 4.4 also highlights that districts with more Tier 3 revenue had higher revenue overall; however, some of the districts with the lowest share of Tier 3 revenue (as a percentage of all revenue) also have relatively high total revenue, so that relationship is not strictly monotonic.

---

[2]   Although the average Tier 3 revenue per pupil for small rural districts also appears high, the difference between those districts and the reference category of large suburbs is not statistically significant.

Table 4.2
ADA-Weighted Revenues per ADA by District Characteristics, California K–12 School Districts, 2007–08 to 2009–10

	Group Statistics		All Revenue per ADA 07–08	All Revenue per ADA 08–09	All Revenue per ADA 09–10	Tier 3 Revenue per ADA 07–08	Tier 3 Revenue per ADA 08–09	Stimulus Revenue per ADA 08–09	Stimulus Revenue per ADA 09–10
	Mean	Number of Districts							
District Type									
Elementary#	516		$9,334	$9,419	$8,609	$468	$383	$457	$90
High school	77		$10,717**	$10,934**	$9,996**	$1,038**	$802**	$594**	$160**
Unified	328		$10,165**	$10,256**	$9,412**	$922**	$748**	$609**	$175**
Unified without LA			$9,761**	$9,856**	$8,985**	$735**	$565**	$542**	$139**
Fiscal Health									
Health#	336		$9,835	$9,896	$9,033	$723	$593	$522	$130
Marginal	403		$10,278**	$10,378**	$9,553**	$942**	$768**	$622**	$179**
Marginal without LA			$9,776	$9,883	$9,028	$703	$535**	$537	$133
Unhealthy	180		$9,644	$9,800	$8,913	$698	$538	$515	$123
Basic Aid Status									
Not Basic Aid#	833		$9,978	$10,068	$9,199	$847	$685	$593	$159
Not Basic Aid without LA			$9,670	$9,763	$8,871	$706	$548	$543	$132
Basic Aid	88		$12,242**	$12,685**	$12,538**	$740	$637	$147**	$83**
Urban Category									
Large city	44		$11,281**	$11,380**	$10,563**	$1,341**	$1,121**	$772**	$266**
Large city without LA			$10,488**	$10,610**	$9,706**	$909**	$677**	$624**	$190**
Small, mid-size city	95		$9,764	$9,840	$9,049	$714	$599*	$507	$124
Large suburb#	195		$9,592	$9,693	$8,812	$673	$530	$512	$116
Small, mid-size suburb	69		$9,021**	$9,143**	$8,239**	$555**	$426*	$481	$101*
Town	164		$9,662	$9,811	$8,965	$665	$474	$530	$130
Rural, metro	290		$9,701	$9,804	$8,911	$554*	$391**	$496	$107
Rural, remote nonmetro	64		$14,398**	$14,803**	$13,765**	$1,067	$802	$572	$148

Table 4.2—Continued

	Group Statistics		All Revenue per ADA 07–08	All Revenue per ADA 08–09	All Revenue per ADA 09–10	Tier 3 Revenue per ADA 07–08	Tier 3 Revenue per ADA 08–09	Stimulus Revenue per ADA 08–09	Stimulus Revenue per ADA 09–10
	Mean	Number of Districts							
Enrollment Size (quintiles)									
1	125	176	$13,535**	$13,590**	$12,850**	$950	$767	$585	$150
2	502	180	$10,810	$11,045	$10,359	$716	$563	$505	$114
3#	1,762	187	$10,103	$10,286	$9,495	$585	$443	$472	$106
4	5,015	189	$9,605*	$9,775	$8,901**	$615	$489	$466	$98
5 (largest)	105,074	189	$10,114	$10,192	$9,345	$913**	$746**	$611**	$174**
5 (largest) without LA	27,801		$10,488*	$10,610**	$9,706**	$909**	$677**	$624**	$190**

\# Reference group; *p<0.1; **p<0.05.

Table 4.3
ADA-Weighted Revenues per ADA by Student Characteristics, California K–12 School Districts, 2007–08 to 2009–10

Quintiles	Group Statistics		All Revenue per ADA 07–08	All Revenue per ADA 08–09	All Revenue per ADA 09–10	Tier 3 Revenue per ADA 07–08	Tier 3 Revenue per ADA 08–09	Stimulus Revenue per ADA 08–09	Stimulus Revenue per ADA 09–10
	Mean	Number of Districts							
API Performance									
1	678	183	$11,145**	$11,248**	$10,368**	$1,239**	$1,056**	$754**	$254**
1 without LA	677	183	$13,535**	$13,590**	$12,850**	$950	$767**	$585**	$150**
2	724	183	$9,848	$9,901	$9,048	$709*	$560	$564*	$147**
3#	761	184	$9,777	$9,921	$9,049	$787	$551	$538	$128
4	798	181	$9,325**	$9,399**	$8,607**	$610**	$500	$472**	$98**
5 (highest API)	864	177	$9,237**	$9,372**	$8,586**	$541**	$423**	$405**	$73**
Percent of Students from Poor Families									
1	11.6%	189	$9,302**	$9,475**	$8,693**	$585**	$476**	$409**	$76**
2	32.2%	193	$9,341**	$9,426**	$8,566**	$658**	$496**	$490**	$104**
3#	48.0%	181	$9,768	$9,943	$9,121	$787	$676	$540	$125
4	63.2%	175	$10,085**	$10,151	$9,212	$739	$511**	$581**	$157**
5 (poorest)	80.9%	183	$11,234**	$11,285**	$10,483**	$1,284**	$1,099**	$773**	$269**
5 (poorest) without LA	83.9%		$10,314**	$10,354**	$9,467*	$758	$625	$609**	$186**
Percent of English Learners									
1	1.3%	194	$10,554**	$10,757**	$9,788**	$687	$542	$467	$101
2	6.6%	179	$9,365	$9,502	$8,708	$585	$489	$440**	$85**
3#	14.3%	183	$9,275	$9,383	$8,549	$672	$502	$508	$112
4	28.1%	185	$10,681**	$10,769**	$9,925**	$1,095**	$902**	$676**	$212**
4 without LA	26.4%		$10,065**	$10,161**	$9,263**	$788**	$605**	$567**	$154**
5 (most EL)	45.1%	180	$10,091**	$10,171**	$9,289**	$711	$573	$566**	$152**

Reference group; *p<0.1; **p<0.05.

Table 4.4
ADA-Weighted Revenues per ADA by Tier 3 Revenue, California K–12 School Districts, 2007–08 to 2009–10

Quintiles	Group Statistics		All Revenue per ADA 07–08	All Revenue per ADA 08–09	All Revenue per ADA 09–10	Tier 3 Revenue per ADA 07–08	Tier 3 Revenue per ADA 08–09	Stimulus Revenue per ADA 08–09	Stimulus Revenue per ADA 09–10
	Mean	Number of Districts							
Tier 3 Revenue per ADA (in 2007–08)									
1	$339	176	$8,574**	$8,744**	$7,896**	$339**	$254**	$424**	$73**
2	$445	189	$9,136	$9,203	$8,450	$445**	$336**	$456**	$99**
3#	$558	186	$9,389	$9,492	$8,574	$558	$428	$492	$116
4	$750	187	$9,939**	$10,021**	$9,143**	$750**	$614**	$560**	$156**
5 (highest)	$1,519	183	$11,645**	$11,752**	$10,940**	$1,519**	$1,195**	$775**	$248**
5 (highest) without LA	$1,256		$11,186**	$11,317**	$10,435**	1,256***	$903**	$652**	$173**
Tier 3 Share of All Revenue (in 2007–08)									
1	3.6%	170	$9,614**	$9,807**	$9,073**	$339**	$292**	$408**	$72**
2	4.6%	187	$9,315	$9,432	$8,614	$430**	$311**	$446**	$94**
3#	5.7%	189	$9,158	$9,230	$8,321	$523	$402	$487	$111
4	7.2%	190	$9,700**	$9,778**	8,926**	$702**	$567**	$553**	$153**
5 (highest)	12.5%	185	$11,292**	11,403**	10,567**	$1,438**	$1,136**	$748**	$234**
5 (highest) without LA	10.9%		$10,741**	10,873**	9,967**	$1,181**	$865**	$632**	$165**

Reference group; *p<0.1; **p<0.05

Revenue Shares

Given that districts with relatively more Tier 3 revenue per pupil also tend to have relatively more total revenue per pupil, one might wonder if the *share* of revenue coming from Tier 3 sources is similar across districts. Table 4.5 shows that this is not the case: There is wide variation across districts in the percentage of revenue that districts receive through Tier 3 programs and through restricted programs more generally. Even in 2009–10, when Tier 3 monies are considered unrestricted, the average student is in a district that has strings attached to 27 percent of its budget.

Tables 4.6 and 4.7 detail the distribution of revenue shares by district characteristics and district-level student characteristics. We see that the variation in Tier 3 revenue share generally follows similar patterns as revenue levels (i.e., the share is higher in high school, large urban, low-performing, and high-poverty districts) but the patterns are not as strong. In particular, when LAUSD is excluded, the difference between the lowest-performing quintile and the middle (reference) quintile largely goes away, and the Tier 3 share in the highest-poverty quintile is actually smaller than in the middle quintile.

Prior to flexibility, in 2007–08, noticeably larger shares of restricted revenue were found more generally in large urban districts and in lower-performing, higher-poverty, and more-EL districts. Unsurprisingly, Basic Aid districts have significantly less restricted revenue. In 2009–10, after Tier 3 flexibility was adopted, large urban, lower-performing, higher-poverty, and more-EL districts still had more restricted revenue, although the differences were not as large and restricted shares were lower across the board. Thus, as expected, all districts gained some flexibility, but that gain was larger for districts that started out with the most restricted budgets in 2007–08.

Table 4.5
ADA-Weighted Revenues Shares, California K–12 School Districts, 2007–08 to 2009–10

	Tier 3 Share of All Revenue 07–08	Tier 3 Share of All Revenue 08–09	Percent Restricted Revenue 07–08	Percent Restricted Revenue 08–09 (Tier 3 Restricted)	Percent Restricted Revenue 08–09 (Tier 3 Unrestricted)	Percent Restricted Revenue 09–10
Mean	8%	6%	30%	32%	26%	27%
Standard deviation	4%	4%	9%	9%	7%	7%
Minimum	1%	0%	3%	2%	1%	1%
Maximum	30%	23%	77%	79%	78%	80%
Number of districts	921	867	921	921	867	921

Table 4.6
ADA-Weighted Revenues Shares by District Characteristics, California K–12 School Districts, 2007–08 to 2009–10

	Group Statistics	Tier 3 Share of All Revenue 07–08	Tier 3 Share of All Revenue 08–09	Percent Restricted Revenue 07–08	Percent Restricted Revenue 08–09 (Tier 3 Restricted)	Percent Restricted Revenue (Tier 3 Unrestricted)	Percent Restricted Revenue 09–10
	Mean Number of Districts						
District Type							
Elementary#	516	5%	4%	26%	28%	24%	26%
High school	77	10%**	7%**	28%	29%	22%**	23%**
Unified	328	9%**	7%**	31%**	33%**	27%**	28%**
Unified without LA		7%**	6%**	29%	31%	26%**	27%**
Fiscal Health							
Health#	336	7%	6%	28%	29%	24%	25%
Marginal	403	9%**	7%**	32%**	33%**	27%**	28%**
Marginal without LA		7%	5%**	29%	30%	26%**	27%**
Unhealthy	180	7%	5%	28%	29%	25%	25%
Basic Aid Status							
Not Basic Aid#	833	8%	6%	30%	32%	26%	27%
Not Basic Aid without LA		7%	5%	29%	30%	25%	26%
Basic Aid	88	6%**	5%**	21%**	20%**	15%**	16%**
Urban Category							
Large city	44	11%**	9%**	38%**	39%**	31%**	32%**
Large city without LA		8%**	6%**	34%**	35%**	30%**	30%**
Small, mid-size city	95	7%	6%**	29%*	30%	25%	26%
Large suburb#	195	7%	5%	27%	29%	24%	25%
Small, mid-size suburb	69	6%*	5%*	24%**	26%**	22%**	23%**
Town	164	7%	5%	27%	29%	24%	25%
Rural, metro	290	6%***	4%**	25%**	26%**	23%*	23%**
Rural, remote nonmetro	64	7%	5%	30%	29%	25%	24%

Table 4.6—Continued

	Group Statistics		Tier 3 Share of All Revenue 07–08	Tier 3 Share of All Revenue 08–09	Percent Restricted Revenue 07–08	Percent Restricted Revenue 08–09 (Tier 3 Restricted)	Percent Restricted Revenue (Tier 3 Unrestricted)	Percent Restricted Revenue 09–10
	Mean	Number of Districts						
Enrollment Size (quintiles)								
1	91	176	7%	5%	26%	27%	22%	21%
2	441	180	6%	5%	25%	27%	22%	22%
3#	1,591	187	6%	4%	25%	26%	22%	23%
4	4,546	189	6%	5%	26%	28%	23%	24%
5 (largest)	21,599	189	9%**	7%**	31%**	33%**	27%**	28%**
5 (largest) without LA			7%**	6%**	29%**	31%**	26%**	27%**

Reference group; *p<0.1; **p<0.05.

Table 4.7
ADA-Weighted Revenues Shares by Student Characteristics, California K–12 School Districts, 2007–08 to 2009–10

	Group Statistics		Tier 3 Share of All Revenue 07–08	Tier 3 Share of All Revenue 08–09	Percent Restricted Revenue 07–08	Percent Restricted Revenue 08–09 (Tier 3 Restricted)	Percent Restricted Revenue (Tier 3 Unrestricted)	Percent Restricted Revenue 09–10
	Mean	Number of Districts						
API Performance								
1	669	183	11%**	9%**	37%**	39%**	30%**	32%**
1 without LA		183	8%	6%**	33%**	35%**	29%**	31%**
2	723	183	7%**	6%	30%	32%*	27%**	28%**
3#	759	184	8%	5%	29%	30%	26%	26%
4	801	181	6%**	5%	25%**	27%**	22%**	23%**
5 (highest API)	870	177	6%**	5%**	22%**	23%**	19%**	20%**
Percent of Students from Poor Families								
1	0.0%	189	6%**	5%**	22%**	23%**	19%**	19%**
2	31.6%	193	7%**	5%**	25%**	27%**	22%**	23%**
3#	47.5%	181	8%	7%	28%	30%	24%	25%
4	63.4%	175	7%**	5%**	32%**	33%**	29%**	30%**
5 (poorest)	87.2%	183	11%**	9%**	38%**	40%**	31%**	33%**
5 (poorest) without LA			7%**	6%**	34%**	36%**	30%**	32%**
Percent of English Learners								
1	0.7%	194	6%	5%	23%	25%	20%*	20%**
2	5.9%	179	6%**	5%	22%**	25%**	20%**	21%**
3#	14.1%	183	7%	5%	25%	27%	22%	23%
4	26.2%	185	10%**	8%**	35%**	36%**	29%**	30%**
4 without LA			8%**	6%**	31%**	33%**	27%**	29%**
5 (most EL)	48.7%	180	7%	6%	33%**	35%**	30%**	31%**

Reference group; *p<0.1; **p<0.05.

Revenue Changes

Given that Tier 3 programs experienced deeper cuts than other programs and that lower-performing and higher-poverty districts receive more Tier 3 funds, some in the education community have raised concerns that the highest-need districts have experienced the largest revenue losses. To assess whether such concern is warranted, Tables 4.8 through 4.12 show changes in Tier 3 and total revenues per pupil for all districts and by district characteristics. What the data seem to reveal is that how one interprets the relative loss between 2007–08 and 2009–10 can depend on whether the focus is dollars or percentage changes and in many cases, there is no clear pattern.

In *dollars*, the biggest drops in Tier 3 revenue per pupil are, not surprisingly, for districts that start out with the most Tier 3 revenue per pupil (high schools; large urban schools; low-performing, high-poverty, more-EL schools); however, for student performance, the largest drop was in the middle quintile, and the differences for size, poverty, and English learners go away when Los Angeles is excluded.

In *percentage* terms, there are few clear patterns to Tier 3 losses. Unified districts and fiscally unhealthy districts have larger percentage reductions in Tier 3. Also, somewhat inexplicably, districts in the middle quintile of API performance and English learners and districts in the fourth quintile of poverty experienced larger percentage drops in Tier 3 revenues per pupil than other districts.

As noted earlier, some of the losses in Tier 3 (and other) funding were balanced out by stimulus funds in 2008–09, so most districts saw increased revenue between 2007–08 and 2008–09. Then, however, there were relatively large drops between 2008–09 and 2009–10, so overall the change from 2007–08 to 2009–10 is definitely negative for all except Basic Aid districts. However, the differences across district characteristics are quite small and only statistically significant in a few cases. From the data in the last column of Table 4.12, it actually appears that districts with more Tier 3 revenue per pupil experienced somewhat *smaller* overall reductions in total revenue per pupil than other districts.

Thus, although all districts are clearly working with reduced budgets relative to 2007–08, there is little evidence that districts serving more higher-need students have been disproportionately affected.

Table 4.8
ADA-Weighted Revenues Shares by Tier 3 Revenue, California K–12 School Districts, 2007–08 to 2009–10

	Group Statistics		Tier 3 Share of All Revenue 07–08	Tier 3 Share of All Revenue 08–09	Percent Restricted Revenue 07–08	Percent Restricted Revenue 08–09 (Tier 3 Restricted)	Percent Restricted Revenue (Tier 3 Unrestricted)	Percent Restricted Revenue 09–10
	Mean	Number of Districts						
Tier 3 Revenue per ADA (in 2007–08)								
1	$337	176	4%**	3%**	21%**	23%**	20%**	21%**
2	$444	189	5%**	4%**	25%**	26%**	23%**	24%
3#	$564	186	6%	5%	27%	29%	25%	25%
4	$764	187	8%**	6%**	30%**	32%**	26%**	28%**
5 (highest)	$1,615	183	13%**	10%**	38%**	39%**	29%**	31%**
5 (highest) without LA			11%**	8%**	35%**	35%**	27%**	29%**
Tier 3 Share of All Revenue (in 2007–08)								
1	3.4%	170	4%**	3%**	23%**	24%**	22%*	23%**
2	4.6%	187	5%**	3%**	25%	26%**	24%	25%
3#	5.7%	189	6%	4%	26%	28%	24%	25%
4	7.2%	190	7%**	6%**	29%**	31%**	26%**	27%**
5 (highest)	11.3%	185	13%**	10%**	37%**	38%**	28%**	30%**
5 (highest) without LA			11%**	8%**	33%**	34%**	27%**	28%**

Reference group; *p<0.1; **p<0.05.

Table 4.9
ADA-Weighted Revenues Changes, California K–12 School Districts, 2007–08 to 2009–10

	Change in Tier 3 Revenue 07–08	Percent Change in Tier 3 Revenue	Change in All Revenue 07–08	Percent Change in All Revenue 07–08	Change in All Revenue (08–09	Percent Change in All Revenue 08–09	Percent Change in All Revenue 07–09
Revenues per ADA							
Mean	–$187	–22%	$101	1.0%	–$846	–8.6%	–7.7%
Standard deviation	$215	22%	$323	2.9%	$452	4.2%	4.5%
Minimum	–$1,946	–99%	–$11,510	–43.9%	–$17,392	–46.7%	–47.3%
Maximum	$1,169	102%	$14,479	63.6%	$14,270	49.9%	58.2%
Number of districts	867	867	921	921	921	921	921

Table 4.10
ADA-Weighted Revenues Changes by District Characteristics, California K–12 School Districts, 2007–08 to 2009–10

	Group Statistics		Change in Tier 3 Revenue 07–08	Percent Change in Tier 3 Revenue	Change in All Revenue 07–08	Percent Change in All Revenue 07–08	Change in All Revenue 08–09	Percent Change in All Revenue 08–09	Percent Change in All Revenue 07–09
	Mean	Number of Districts							
District Type									
Elementary#		516	-$91	-19%	$85	1.0%	-$810	-8.9%	-8.0%
High school		77	-$237**	-22%	$217**	2.0%**	-$937**	-8.7%	-7.0%**
Unified		328	-$205**	-23%**	$91	0.9%	-$844	-8.5%	-7.6%
Unified without LA			-$191**	-25%**	$95**	1.0%	-$871**	-9.0%	-8.1%*
Fiscal Health									
Healthy#		336	-$150	-20%	$60	0.6%	-$862	-8.9%	-8.4%
Marginal		403	-$206**	-22%	$100	1.0%	-$825	-8.2%**	-7.3%**
Marginal without LA			-$189**	-24%**	$108*	1.1%**	-$856	-8.8%	-7.8%
Unhealthy		180	-$172	-28%**	$156**	1.6%**	-$888	-9.2%	-7.8%
Basic Aid Status									
Not Basic Aid#		833	-$189	-23%	$90	0.9%	-$869	-8.8%	-8.0%
Not Basic Aid without LA			-$177	-24%	$93	1.0%	-$891	-9.2%	-8.4%
Basic Aid		88	-$120**	-16%	$443**	3.7%**	-$147**	-1.4%**	2.2%**
Urban Category									
Large city		44	-$279**	-21%	$100	0.9%	-$817	-7.3%**	-6.5%**
Large city without LA			-$282	-26%	$122	1.1%	-$904	-8.6%	-7.5%*
Small, mid-size city		95	-$135	-19%**	476	0.8%	-$791**	-8.2%**	-7.5%*
Large suburb#		195	-$155	-23%	4100	1.1%	-$880	-9.2%	-8.3%
Small, mid-size suburb		69	-$142	-25%	$122	1.3%	-$904	-10.1%*	-8.9%
Town		164	-$189	-28%	$149	1.5%	-$846	-8.8%	-7.5%
Rural, metro		290	-$176	-30%*	$102	1.3%	-$893	-9.5%	-8.4%
Rural, remote nonmetro		64	-$261	-26%	$405	2.9%	-$1,038	-6.9%	-4.4%

Table 4.10—Continued

	Group Statistics		Change in Tier 3 Revenue 07–08	Percent Change in Tier 3 Revenue	Change in All Revenue 07–08	Percent Change in All Revenue 07–08	Change in All Revenue 08–09	Percent Change in All Revenue 08–09	Percent Change in All Revenue 07–09
	Mean	Number of Districts							
Enrollment Size (quintiles)									
1	125	176	–$193	–21%	$55	1.5%	–$740	–5.8%	–5.0%
2	502	180	–$159	–21%	$236	2.2%	–$686	–6.7%	–4.8%
3#	1,762	187	–$148	–25%	$183	1.8%	–$791	–8.1%	–6.5%
4	5,015	189	–$127	–20%	$170	1.7%	–$875	–9.2%*	–7.7%*
5 (largest)	10,5074	189	–$203*	–23%	$79**	0.8%**	–$847	–8.5%	–7.8%**
5 (largest) without LA			–$193	–21%	$55**	1.5%**	–$740	–5.8%	–5.0%**

Reference group; *p<0.1; **p<0.05.

Table 4.11
ADA-Weighted Revenues Changes by Student Characteristics, California K–12 School Districts, 2007–08 to 2009–10

	Group Statistics		Change in Tier 3 Revenue 07–08	Percent Change in Tier 3 Revenue	Change in All Revenue 07–08	Percent Change in All Revenue 07–08	Change in All Revenue 08–09	Percent Change in All Revenue 08–09	Percent Change in All Revenue 07–09
	Mean	Number of Districts							
API Performance									
1	678	183	−$204**	−18%***	$103	1.0%	−$880	−8.0%**	−7.2%
1 without LA			−$162**	−20%***	$123	1.2%	−985**	−9.4%	−8.4%*
2	724	183	−$169**	−23%***	$53**	0.6%**	−$853	−8.9%	−8.3%
3#	761	184	−$268	−32%	$144	1.4%	−$873	−8.9%	−7.6%
4	798	181	−$126**	−20%***	$73**	0.8%*	−$792	−8.7%	−8.0%
5 (highest API)	864	177	−$131**	−23%***	$135	1.4%	−$787*	−8.7%	−7.4%
Percent of Students from Poor Families									
1	11.6%	189	−$130	−21%	$173	1.8%	−$782	−8.6%	−7.0%
2	32.2%	193	−$170	−26%***	$85**	1.0%**	−$860	−9.3%***	−8.5%**
3#	48.0%	181	−$138	−18%	$176	1.7%	−$822	−8.4%	−6.9%
4	63.2%	175	−$257**	−30%***	$65**	0.7%***	−$939***	−9.4%***	−8.8%***
5 (poorest)	80.9%	183	−$200**	−16%	$52**	0.5%**	−$802	−7.3%***	−6.9%
5 (poorest) without LA			−$140	−18%	$40**	0.4%**	−$887	−8.6%	−8.3%**
Percent of English Learners									
1	1.3%	194	−$144	−22%	$203	2.1%	−$969	−8.8%	−7.1%
2	6.6%	179	−$116**	−20%**	$137	1.4%	−4794	−8.9%	−7.6%
3#	14.3%	183	−$184	−28%	$108	1.2%	−$834	−9.0%	−8.0%
4	28.1%	185	−$225**	−21%***	$88	0.8%	−4845	−8.1%**	−7.3%
4 without LA			−$207	−23%**	$96	1.0%	−$898	−9.0%	−8.1%*
5 (most ELs)	45.1%	180	−$154	−22%**	$80	0.8%	−$882	−8.8%	−8.2%

Reference group; *p<0.1; **p<0.05.

Table 4.12
ADA-Weighted Revenues Changes by Tier 3 Revenue, California K–12 School Districts, 2007–08 to 2009–10

	Group Statistics		Change in Tier 3 Revenue 07–08	Percent Change in Tier 3 Revenue	Change in All Revenue 07–08	Percent Change in All Revenue 07–08	Change in All Revenue 08–09	Percent Change in All Revenue 08–09	Percent Change in All Revenue 07–09
	Mean	Number of Districts							
Tier 3 Revenue per ADA (07–08)									
1	$339	176	–$90*	–25%	$170*	2.0%**	–$848	–9.8%	–8.1%
2	$445	189	–$110	–25%	$67	0.8%	–$753**	–8.4%**	–7.7%**
3#	$558	186	–$132	–23%	$103	1.1%	–$918	–9.9%	–8.9%
4	$750	187	–$138	–19%**	$82	0.8%	–$879	–8.7%**	–8.0%**
5 (highest)	$1,519	183	–$325**	–23%	$108	0.9%	–$812**	–7.0%**	–6.2%**
5 (highest) without LA			–$353**	–28%**	$131	1.2%	–$882	–7.9%**	–6.9%**
Tier 3 Share of All revenue (07–08)									
1	3.6%	170	–$58**	–17%**	$193**	2.0%**	–$734**	–8.4%**	–6.5%**
2	4.6%	187	–$122	–28%	$118	1.2%	–$818*	–8.8%**	–7.7%**
3#	5.7%	189	–$122	–24%	$72	0.8%	–$909	–9.9%	–9.2%
4	7.2%	190	–$139	–20%	$77	0.8%	–$852	–8.8%**	–8.0%**
5 (highest)	12.5%	185	–$304**	–22%	$111	1.0%	–$836*	–7.5%**	–6.6%**
5 (highest) without LA			–$318**	–26%	$132*	1.2%	–$906	–8.4%**	–7.3%**

Reference group; *p<0.1; **p<0.05.

CHAPTER FIVE

Spending Priorities

One of the big questions about increased local control in general is what sort of changes districts will make when given the opportunity—in particular, whether they will continue to meet the needs of the students whom categorical programs were originally intended to serve. As discussed in Chapter Three, although it is difficult with statewide data to identify district spending on specific programs, we can examine broad priorities by looking at what items districts are buying and how they distribute spending across various types of educational goals, as well as whether there have been changes in those spending patterns since the Tier 3 flexibility policy was adopted. The key questions of interest here are the following:

- How do districts spend Tier 3 dollars?[1]
- How do they spend total overall revenue?
- Do districts with larger shares of Tier 3 funding have different spending patterns, particularly for instruction and teaching staff, compared to those with less Tier 3 funding?

Tier 3 and Total Expenditures

Table 5.1 shows the average percentage of district budgets, both overall and Tier 3 money, allocated to the seven function-object categories and to the eight goal categories. Table 5.2 shows the average dollars per pupil in each category.

In both 2007–08 and 2008–09, the majority of Tier 3 funds were spent on direct instruction, with a slight shift toward personnel (salaries and benefits) over other items after flexibility was adopted. Note that the level of Tier 3 spending went down in all categories, so any changes in expenditure shares are coming from relative differences in the size of the drop in different categories. The majority of total spending is also devoted to direct instruction. It is worth noting that a substantial share of Tier 3 money is being used to buy materials, but those materials are a relatively small share of the overall budget.

The goal categories show that the majority of Tier 3 and overall funding is used for general K–12 education. The share of Tier 3 monies going to alternative and adult education is higher than the share of the overall budget spent on those categories, and those Tier 3 shares increased in 2008–09, but the overall levels are still small. The changes in expenditure shares over time are not large; for overall spending, there is a slight decrease in the relative share

---

[1] Keep in mind that Tier 3 dollars cannot be identified in the SACS after 2008–09.

Table 5.1
ADA-Weighted Expenditure Shares, California K–12 School Districts, 2007–08 to 2009–10

	07–08 Tier 3	08–09 Tier 3	07–08	08–09	09–10
All Expenditures per ADA	$672	$542	$11,243	$11,013	$10,776
Function-Object Categories					
Instructional salaries and benefits	34%	35%	54%	55%	55%
Other instruction	26%	25%	7.2%	6.3%	6.0%
Instruction-related salaries and benefits	15%	16%	11%	11%	11%
Other instruction-related	3.7%	3.1%	1.7%	1.5%	1.3%
Pupil services	11%	11%	7.5%	7.5%	7.5%
LEA administration	3.0%	2.8%	6.3%	6.3%	6.4%
All other	7.8%	7.7%	13%	13%	13%
Goal Categories					
Undistributed	18%	16%	25%	27%	24%
Pre-kindergarten	0.1%	0.1%	0.8%	1.0%	1.0%
General K–12 education	58%	53%	54%	57%	53%
Alternative education	5.6%	8%	1.8%	1.0%	1.8%
Adult education	13%	16%	1.3%	1.0%	1.1%
Supplemental education	0.5%	0.6%	1.1%	0.0%	1.0%
Special education	0.2%	0.2%	15%	11%	16%
Other goals	5.2%	5.5%	2.0%	2.0%	1.8%

devoted to instructional materials and a slight increase in the relative share for district administration and special education.

It is perhaps easier to see certain district priorities by looking at changes in average per-pupil spending levels. The last column of Table 5.2 contains the percentage change in per-pupil spending from 2007–08 to 2009–10. Overall, spending fell by 4.3 percent, but the drop was larger in some categories and smaller in others, indicating which categories districts protected as budgets were tightened. Districts appear to have maintained instructional personnel, pupil services, district administration, pre-kindergarten, and special education more than other areas. In contrast, instructional and instruction-related materials, and alternative and adult education, appear to have taken relatively larger hits. This seems consistent with the findings of Fuller et al. (2011) that many districts tried to protect core programs.

Table 5.2
ADA-Weighted Expenditures per Pupil, California K-12 School Districts, 2007–08 to 2009–10

	07–08 Tier 3 Expenditures	08–09 Tier 3 Expenditures	07–08 Expenditures	08–09 Expenditures	09–10 Expenditures	Percentage Change, 07–09
All Expenditures per ADA	$778	$640	$10,238	$10,098	$9,787	–4.3%
Function–Object Categories						
Instructional salaries and benefits	$296	$248	$5,433	$5,449	$5,332	–1.7%
Other instruction	$156	$112	$742	$640	$598	–19.9%
Instruction-related salaries and benefits	$111	$97	$1,130	$1,108	$1,050	–6.1%
Other instruction-related	$27	$19	$180	$155	$132	–19.1%
Pupil services	$94	$84	$770	$766	$743	–2.8%
LEA administration	$23	$21	$638	$635	$623	–2.0%
All other	$70	$58	$1,346	$1,344	$1,309	–2.8%
Goal Categories						
Undistributed	$120	$92	$2,508	$2,474	$2,355	–5%
Pre-kindergarten	$0.86	$0.69	$92	$95	$108	18.5%
General K-12 education	$426	$330	$5,453	$5,334	$5,103	–6%
Alternative education	$53	$51	$185	$184	$178	–1.8%
Adult education	$126	$119	$147	$146	$119	–13.9%
Supplemental education	$2.56	$1.84	$116	$99	$99	–1.3%
Special education	$1.87	$1.55	$1,526	$1,566	$1,638	11%
Other goals	$47	$44	$210	$199	$187	–0.6%

Distribution of Spending

Given the differences in which districts receive more Tier 3 funding, and the differences in how districts spend Tier 3 funds relative to all other funding, it is reasonable to expect districts with more Tier 3 funding to have different spending patterns than other districts. Those patterns are shown in Tables 5.3 to 5.6, which divide districts into quintiles based on their Tier 3 revenue per pupil in 2007–08. Tables 5.4 and 5.6 show the dollar amount of spending in each cell; since districts with more Tier 3 revenue also have more total expenditures, they spend more in almost every category. The focus here is primarily on the percentage shares in Tables 5.3 and 5.5 (that is, the share of spending in each category), indicating the relative priority that districts give to various functions and goals.

A few striking patterns emerge. Relative to districts with low levels of Tier 3 revenue per pupil, districts with more Tier 3 funding spend a much larger share of those funds on instructional personnel and "all other" functions (which includes maintenance and community services) and a smaller share on other instruction items such as books and materials. The difference between high– and low–Tier 3 districts in their instructional share is not quite as large when Los Angeles is excluded, but there is still a noticeable difference. Districts with more Tier 3 revenue per pupil also spend relatively more of their Tier 3 funds on alternative education, adult education, and noninstructional goals, and relatively less on general K–12 education. None of these spending patterns appears to change much from 2007–08 to 2008–09, although the middle quintile shows a particularly large jump in the share of Tier 3 funds spent on alternative education in 2008–09.

Although districts with more Tier 3 revenue per pupil spend relatively more Tier 3 money on instructional personnel, they spend a smaller share of their *overall* budgets on this category.[2] Instead, relatively more of their total budget goes to pupil services and "all other" functions, compared to districts with less Tier 3 funding. However, from 2007–08 to 2009–10, all districts spend a slightly larger share on instructional personnel and a slightly smaller share on instructional materials.

Among the goal categories, priorities for the total budget appear to match the goals for Tier 3, with higher–Tier 3 districts devoting relatively more of their budgets than lower–Tier 3 districts to alternative education, adult education, and other goals, as well as special education, and relatively less on general K–12 education.

So districts with larger shares of Tier 3 funding do spend relatively more of their Tier 3 funding on instruction and teaching staff than districts with less Tier 3 funding, but they spend less of their *total* budget on instruction and teaching staff. This is perhaps unsurprising when one considers that districts with larger shares of Tier 3 funding also tend to have more students with higher needs (e.g., lower-performing, higher-poverty students), and they must devote more of their budgets to such pupil services such as counseling, health, and food. One interpretation of these patterns is that the reduction of Tier 3 funds may mean these districts are harder-pressed than other districts to protect their instructional staff as budgets fall. Tables 5.7 and 5.8 try to clarify whether districts made different choices about which categories to protect by showing the percentage change in spending in each category between 2007–08 and 2009–10. Given the overall reduction in funding (shown in the first column), smaller (or

---

[2]   Recall that these districts do generally have larger budgets, so although the budget shares are smaller, the per-pupil dollar amounts are not necessarily smaller.

Table 5.3
ADA-Weighted Function Expenditure Shares, by Tier 3 Revenue

Quintiles of Tier 3 Revenue per ADA	Expenditures per ADA	Instructional Salaries and Benefits	Other Instruction	Instruction-Related Salaries and Benefits	Other Instruction-Related	Pupil Services	LEA Administration	All Other
Tier 3 Expenditures, 2007–08								
1	$340	27%	42%**	13%**	3.5%**	9%**	2.7%*	3%**
2	$445	32%**	33%**	15%*	3.2%**	9%**	3.4%*	4%**
3#	$556	29%	29%	16%	5.1%	11%	3.1%	6%
4	$740	34%**	25%**	16%	3.4%**	10%	2.9%	9%**
5 (highest)	$1,502	41%**	14%**	14%**	3.2%**	13%**	3.0%	12%**
5 (highest) without LA	$1,241	35%**	18%**	15%*	3.8%**	11%	3.2%	14%**
Tier 3 Expenditures, 2008–09								
1	$344	30%	41%**	15%	2.1%**	8%**	2.2%	2%**
2	$447	33%	31%**	17%*	2.4%**	8%**	2.7%**	5%
3#	$558	31%	28%	15%	5.1%	12%	2.2%	7%
4	$745	35%**	22%**	17%**	2.9%**	11%	3.1%**	9%**
5 (highest)	$1,506	39%**	17%**	14%	2.6%**	13%*	3.3%**	11%**
5 (highest) without LA	$1,248	33%	22%**	15%	3.5%**	11%	2.7%**	13%**
All Expenditures, 2007–08								
1	$8,731	57%**	7.3%	9.5%**	1.0%**	6.4%**	6.5%	12%
2	$9,210	56%**	7.2%	9.9%**	1.0%**	6.9%**	6.6%	12%**
3#	$9,483	54%	7.2%	10.4%	1.3%	7.6%	6.3%	13%
4	$10,053	54%	7.3%	10.7%**	1.5%**	7.1%**	6.3%	13%
5 (highest)	$11,958	50%**	7.1%	12.3%**	2.5%**	8.3%**	5.9%*	14%
5 (highest) without LA	$11,407	50%**	6.7%**	11.3%**	2.3%**	8.7%**	6.3%	15%**

Table 5.3—Continued

Quintiles of Tier 3 Revenue per ADA	Expenditures per ADA	Instructional Salaries and Benefits	Other Instruction	Instruction-Related Salaries and Benefits	Other Instruction-Related	Pupil Services	LEA Administration	All Other
All Expenditures, 2008–09								
1	$8,628	58%**	6.1%	9.4%**	0.9%**	6.6%**	6.4%	12%
2	$9,182	58%***	6.3%	9.9%**	0.9%**	6.9%***	6.3%	12%*
3#	$9,291	56%	6.3%	10.3%	1.2%	7.6%	6.4%	13%
4	$9,934	55%**	6.3%	10.6%*	1.3%	7.2%*	6.4%	14%**
5 (highest)	$11,808	51%***	6.3%	12.3%***	2.2%**	8.4%***	6.1%**	14%***
5 (highest) without LA	$11,300	51%***	6.0%	11.3%***	2.2%***	8.9%***	6.2%*	15%***
All Expenditures, 2009–10								
1	$8,302	59%***	5.8%	9.4%***	0.8%**	6.5%	6.6%	12%*
2	$8,875	58%***	6.1%	9.9%*	0.9%***	7.0%	6.5%	12%**
3#	$9,019	56%	5.8%	10.2%	1.1%	7.7%	6.4%	13%
4	$9,680	55%*	5.8%	10.5%**	1.1%	7.3%	6.5%	14%
5 (highest)	$11,496	52%***	6.4%**	11.8%***	1.9%**	8.3%	6.1%	14%***
5 (highest) without LA	$10,956	52%**	5.6%	11.3%***	2.0%**	8.9%	6.2%	15%***

Reference group; *p<0.1; **p<0.05.

Table 5.4
ADA-Weighted Function Expenditures per Pupil, by Tier 3 Revenue

Quintiles of Tier 3 Revenue per ADA	Expenditures per ADA	Instructional Salaries and Benefits	Other Instruction	Instruction-Related Salaries and Benefits	Other Instruction-Related	Pupil Services	LEA Administration	All Other
Tier 3 Expenditures, 2007–08								
1	$340	$87**	$130	$40**	$11**	$30**	$8**	$8**
2	$445	$134	$132	$61**	$13**	$37**	$14	$17
3#	$556	$143	$141	$77	$25	$52	$15	$30
4	$740	$234**	$169	$108**	$24	$70**	$20**	$66**
5 (highest)	$1,502	$606**	$179**	$189**	$43**	$193**	$41**	$150**
5 (highest) without LA	$1,241	$407**	$202**	$176**	$47**	$130**	$38**	$163**
Tier 3 Expenditures, 2008–09								
1	$344	$63**	$78**	$29**	$5**	$19**	$5	$4**
2	$447	$95	$90	$46*	$8**	$28*	$8	$14
3#	$558	$108	$95	$58	$19	$43	$8	$26
4	$745	$205**	$125**	$98**	$18	$66**	$19**	$53**
5 (highest)	$1,506	$517**	$137**	$171**	$31**	$174**	$45**	$122**
5 (highest) without LA	$1,248	$324**	$147**	$153**	$38**	$104**	$28**	$131**
All Expenditures, 2007–08								
1	$8,731	$4,956**	$643	$832**	$91**	$560**	$570	$1,078**
2	$9,210	$5,186	$664	$916**	$97**	$632**	$611	$1,104**
3#	$9,483	$5,099	$686	$984	$126	$718	$600	$1,271
4	$10,053	$5,376**	$733*	$1,080**	$154**	$718	$637**	$1,354
5 (highest)	$11,958	$6,003**	$861**	$1,483**	$309**	$990**	$703**	$1,608**
5 (highest) without LA	$11,407	$5,641**	$767**	$1,293**	$271**	$1,005**	$721**	$1,708**

Table 5.4—Continued

Quintiles of Tier 3 Revenue per ADA	Expenditures per ADA	Instructional Salaries and Benefits	Other Instruction	Instruction-Related Salaries and Benefits	Other Instruction-Related	Pupil Services	LEA Administration	All Other
All Expenditures, 2008–09								
1	$8,628	$4,995*	$536	$817**	$81**	$568**	$556	$1,076
2	$9,182	$5,237	$586	$907*	$88**	$629**	$580	$1,155
3#	$9,291	$5,135	$586	$959	$112	$708	$592	$1,198
4	$9,934	$5,391**	$627	$1,057**	$126	$714	$637**	$1,383**
5 (highest)	$11,808	$5,991**	$754**	$1,465**	$270**	$991**	$723**	$1,614**
5 (highest) without LA	$11,300	$5,685**	$685**	$1,285**	$252**	$1,016**	$702**	$1,676**
All Expenditures, 2009–10								
1	$8,302	$4,864*	$489	$780**	$69**	$541**	$549	$1,009**
2	$8,875	$5,125*	$544	$876	$80*	$616**	$578	$1,057**
3#	$9,019	$4,992	$525	$916	$100	$689	$580	$1,218
4	$9,680	$5,310**	$567*	$1,020**	$112	$705	$632**	$1,333
5 (highest)	$11,496	$5,893**	$749**	$1,370**	$222**	$957**	$701**	$1,604**
5 (highest) without LA	$10,956	$5,596**	$615**	$1,250**	$224**	$978**	$677**	$1,616**

Reference group; *p<0.1; **p<0.05.

Table 5.5
ADA-Weighted Goal Expenditure Shares, by Tier 3 Revenue

Quintiles of Tier 3 Revenue per ADA	Expenditures per ADA	Undistributed	Pre-K	General K-12	Alternative Education	Adult Education	Supplemental Education	Special Education	Other Goals
Tier 3 Expenditures, 2007–08									
1	$340	16%**	0.0%**	78%**	2.2%**	1%***	0.4%*	0.2%	1.0%**
2	$445	20%	0.1%	68%***	5.0%	3%***	0.5%	0.2%	3.0%**
3#	$556	22%	0.2%	59%	5.9%	8%	0.7%	0.1%	4.7%
4	$740	17%**	0.2%	53%**	5.6%	18%***	0.5%	0.2%	6.1%**
5 (highest)	$1,502	15%***	0.1%*	49%***	7.0%*	21%***	0.2%**	0.2%	7.4%***
5 (highest) without LA		22%	0.2%	41%***	4.3%**	24%***	0.4%**	0.3%**	7.0%**
Tier 3 Expenditures, 2008–09									
1	$344	13%***	0.0%**	73%***	5.3%***	6%	1.5%	0.2%	0.8%**
2	$447	19%	0.0%*	60%***	5.9%***	11%	0.4%	0.1%	3.6%*
3#	$558	21%	0.1%	52%	10.6%	10%	1.0%	0.2%	5.2%
4	$745	17%**	0.2%**	47%***	7.1%***	21%***	0.4%	0.1%	6.3%
5 (highest)	$1,506	12%**	0.1%	48%*	8.8%	23%***	0.2%**	0.2%	7.8%***
5 (highest) without LA	$1,248	19%*	0.1%	41%***	6.2%***	26%***	0.3%	0.3%	7.4%**
All Expenditures, 2007–08									
1	$8,731	25%	0.4%**	58%***	0.7%***	0.1%**	0.7%***	13%**	2.0%*
2	$9,210	25%	0.5%*	57%***	1.2%***	0.2%**	0.8%***	14%	1.7%
3#	$9,483	26%	0.7%	54%	1.5%	0.5%	1.3%	15%	1.5%
4	$10,053	24%**	0.6%	55%***	2.0%***	1.4%***	0.9%***	14%	2.0%**
5 (highest)	$11,958	25%**	1.4%**	49%***	2.5%***	2.9%***	1.4%	16%**	2.4%***
5 (highest) without LA		28%**	1.3%**	48%***	2.3%***	3.0%***	1.0%	14%	2.6%**

Table 5.5—Continued

Quintiles of Tier 3 Revenue per ADA	Expenditures per ADA	Undistributed	Pre-K	General K-12	Alternative Education	Adult Education	Supplemental Education	Special Education	Other Goals
All Expenditures, 2008–09									
1	$8,628	25%	0.4%**	58%**	0.7%**	0.1%**	0.7%**	14%**	1.6%
2	$9,182	25%	0.5%**	56%**	1.2%**	0.2%**	0.9%	15%	1.7%
3#	$9,291	26%	0.8%	54%	1.5%	0.5%	1.1%	15%	1.5%
4	$9,934	24%**	0.6%	55%	2.0%**	1.4%**	0.7%**	15%	2.0%**
5 (highest)	$11,808	25%	1.5%**	49%**	2.5%**	2.9%**	1.2%	16%**	2.4%**
5 (highest) without LA	$11,300	28%**	1.4%**	48%**	2.3%**	3.1%**	1.0%	14%	2.6%**
All Expenditures, 2009–10									
1	$8,302	25%	0.5%**	57%**	0.7%**	0.1%**	0.6%**	15%**	1.4%
2	$8,875	24%	0.5%**	56%**	1.1%**	0.1%**	0.9%**	16%	1.7%
3#	$9,019	25%	0.8%	53%	1.5%	0.4%	1.3%	16%	1.4%
4	$9,680	24%**	0.7%	54%	2.0%**	1.3%**	0.7%**	16%	2.1%**
5 (highest)	$11,496	24%*	1.8%**	48%**	2.5%**	2.4%**	1.2%	18%**	2.2%**
5 (highest) without LA	$10,956	27%**	1.5%**	48%**	2.3%**	2.5%**	1.0%**	16%	2.6%**

Reference group; *p<0.1; **p<0.05.

Table 5.6
ADA-Weighted Goal Expenditures per Pupil, by Tier 3 Revenue

Quintiles of Tier 3 Revenue per ADA	Expenditures per ADA	Undistributed	Pre-K	General K–12	Alternative Education	Adult Education	Supplemental Education	Special Education	Other Goals
Tier 3 Expenditures, 2007–08									
1	$340	$52**	$0*	$245	$7**	$5**	$1*	$1	$3**
2	$445	$84	$0	$275	$22	$11*	$2	$1	$13
3#	$556	$105	$1	$284	$30	$37	$3	$1	$22
4	$740	$117	$1	$364**	$40	$121**	$3	$2	$41**
5 (highest)	$1,502	$176**	$1	$712**	$111**	$291**	$2	$4**	$103**
5 (highest) without LA	$1,241	$271**	$2**	$472**	$52**	$279**	$4	$6**	$78**
Tier 3 Expenditures, 2008–09									
1	$344	$30**	$0	$159	$6**	$4*	$1	$0	$2**
2	$447	$59	$0	$190	$18	$9	$1	$0	$12
3#	$558	$80	$1	$197	$25	$31	$2	$1	$21
4	$745	$105**	$2**	$279**	$41	$118**	$2	$1	$37**
5 (highest)	$1,506	$127**	$1	$586**	$108**	$276**	$2	$4**	$94**
5 (highest) without LA	$1,248	$197**	$1	$346**	$43**	$261**	$3**	$6**	$67**
All Expenditures, 2007–08									
1	$8,731	$2,154**	$36**	$5,079	$59**	$6**	$66**	$1,14**6	$183
2	$9,210	$2,285	$45*	$5,214	$104**	$15*	$71**	$1,315	$162
3#	$9,483	$2,444	$71	$5,095	$137	$47	$119	$1,425	$146
4	$10,053	$2,346	$60	$5,573**	$201**	$140**	$91**	$1,432	$210**
5 (highest)	$11,958	$2,917**	$174**	$5,865**	$293**	$339**	$172**	$1,911**	$287**
5 (highest) without LA	$11,407	$3,227**	$152**	$5,408**	$263**	$336**	$121	$1,593**	$307**

Table 5.6—Continued

Quintiles of Tier 3 Revenue per ADA	Expenditures per ADA	Undistributed	Pre-K	General K–12	Alternative Education	Adult Education	Supplemental Education	Special Education	Other Goals
All Expenditures, 2008–09									
1	$8,628	$2,162**	$40**	$4,975	$61**	$7**	$61**	$1,181**	$141
2	$9,182	$2,226	$45**	$5,121	$103**	$14**	$85	$1,432	$157
3#	$9,291	$2,381	$74	$5,008	$137	$47	$101	$1,402	$140
4	$9,934	$2,342	$64	$5,429**	$201**	$143**	$71**	$1,485	$200**
5 (highest)	$11,808	$2,885**	$181**	$5,733**	$292**	$338**	$140**	$1,955**	$284**
5 (highest) without LA	$11,300	$3,135**	$160**	$5,368**	$256**	$340**	$110	$1,627**	$305**
All Expenditures, 2009–10									
1	$8,302	$2,065*	$45**	$4,742	$61**	$5*	$52**	$1,214**	$118
2	$8,875	$2,124	$44**	$4,931	$98**	$11*	$74**	$1,435	$158
3#	$9,019	$2,246	$81	$4,768	$132	$35	$116	$1,512	$129
4	$9,680	$2,287	$72	$5,187**	$193**	$125**	$68	$1,546	$201**
5 (highest)	$11,496	$2,725**	$213**	$5,514**	$287**	$277**	$142**	$2,075**	$262**
5 (highest) without LA	$10,956	$2,955**	$173**	$5,185**	$247**	$269**	$107	$1,724**	$296**

Reference group; *p<0.1; **p<0.05

Table 5.7
ADA-Weighted Percentage Change in Expenditures, 2007–08 to 2009–10, by Tier 3 Revenue

Quintiles of Tier 3 Revenue per ADA	Expenditures per ADA	Instructional Salaries and Benefits	Other Instruction	Instruction-Related Salaries and Benefits	Other Instruction-Related	Pupil Services	LEA Administration	All Other
Percentage Change in All Expenditures, 2007–08 to 2009–10								
1	-4.8%	-1.8%	-25%	-5.5%	-9%*	-2.5%	-3.6%	-5.5%
2	-3.7%**	-1.2%	-18%**	-4.4%**	-7%**	-1.2%	-4.7%	-4.3%
3#	-4.9%	-2.0%	-23%	-6.8%	-18%	-3.1%	-3.5%	-4.7%
4	-4.0%	-1.4%	-22%	-6.1%	-22%	-2.4%	-1.3%**	-0.8%**
5 (highest)	-4.2%	-1.9%	-15%**	-6.7%	-28%**	-3.7%	0.7%**	-1.1%**
5 (highest) without LA	-4.4%	-1.0%**	-21%	-3.1%**	-20%	-3.3%	-4.8%	-7.9%**

Reference group; *p<0.1; **p<0.05.

Table 5.8
ADA-Weighted Percentage Change in Goal Expenditure Shares, 2007–08 to 2009–10

Quintiles of Tier 3 Revenue per ADA	Expenditures per ADA	Undistributed	Pre-K	General K–12	Alternative Education	Adult Education	Supplemental Education	Special Education	Other Goals
Percentage Change in All Expenditures, 2007–08 to 2009–10									
1	–4.8%	2.1%**	80%	–6.4%	–1.7%	–5%**	14%	6.3%	–12%
2	–3.7%	–7.3%	–3%	–5.6%**	–5.8%**	–12%	9%	9.4%	0.2%
3#	–4.9%	–6.1%	16%	–6.9%	3.2%	–14%	–4%	6.8%	–3.5%
4	–4.0%	–3.7%	6%	–6.6%	–3.0%**	–20%**	–2%	10%	1.6%
5 (highest)	–4.2%	–6.4%	19%	–5.7%**	–2.5%**	–13%	–10%	17%**	3.6%
5 (highest) without LA	–4.4%	–8.7%	10%	–4.1%**	–5.9%**	–12%	–3%	21%**	16%**

Reference group; *p<0.1; **p<0.05.

larger) reductions for a particular category can give an indication that districts tried (or did not try) to protect that category.

The function categories in Table 5.7 reflect that, across the board, districts did protect instructional personnel, generally at the expense of instructional materials and instructionally related activities. Districts with more Tier 3 revenue per pupil also appear to have protected district administration and the "all other" category, but that is driven entirely by Los Angeles; when LAUSD is excluded, quintile 5 shows substantially larger reductions in both those categories.

The patterns for the goal categories in Table 5.8 are a bit more complicated. All districts protected (and even increased spending on) special education and pre-K, but high–Tier 3 districts protected special education much more than low–Tier 3 districts did. They also protected noninstructional goals, and the differences for both special education and other goals are even larger when LAUSD is excluded. At the same time, districts with the least Tier 3 revenue were more likely to protect adult education, while quintile 4 shows an unusually large drop in that category.[3]

---

[3]   Although there also appear to be large differences in how districts dealt with pre-K and supplemental education, those differences are not statistically significant, in part because there are a large number of districts without any spending in those categories and a few outliers in quintile 1 with unusually large changes.

CHAPTER SIX

Conclusion

This report set out to address several questions related to the level and distribution of Tier 3 revenues per pupil and the level and distribution of district spending across various components of their budgets. The data show that districts serving larger proportions of high-need students (i.e., low-performing, in poverty, English learners) tend to have higher levels and shares of Tier 3 funding, leading to questions about whether those districts have suffered relatively more from the accompanying funding cuts. Some critics of categorical flexibility have also raised concerns that without the specific program requirements, districts will shift funds away from the high-need students that the programs were intended to serve.

The data here may serve both to allay and increase those concerns. Almost all districts have lost revenue over the past few years, but districts with more Tier 3 funding have lost a similar share of their total budget (though higher dollars per pupil) as other districts, while gaining somewhat more flexibility. So far and on average, districts do not appear to be making large-scale changes in how they are spending their funds. As budgets have shrunk, districts are clearly trying to protect instructional personnel and special education programs. Although there is a lot of variation in how districts have responded to the budget cuts and the Tier 3 flexibility, that variation does not seem to be strongly correlated with any observable district characteristics.

These observations might be some comfort to those who have feared that higher-need districts would be disproportionately hurt by budget cuts or that districts would simply abandon programs for higher-need students without the requirements of the categorical program regulations. On the other hand, districts with comparatively more Tier 3 revenue per pupil do seem to have made relatively larger cuts in programs for alternative and adult education, so the impact on students in these programs is unclear.

The specific research questions, and key findings relative to those questions, include the following:

- **Revenue Levels.** How much total and per-pupil revenue do districts receive through Tier 3 and federal stimulus programs? How have these levels changed over time?
  - **Key findings.** Revenue went up slightly from 2007–08 to 2008–09 (0.5 percent overall) because federal stimulus money filled in for a drop in state funds. However, the stimulus funds were largely allocated in 2008–09, so revenue in 2009–10 dropped 10 percent overall.
- **Distribution of Revenue Levels.** Which districts have received the most Tier 3 and stimulus dollars per pupil? Are there identifiable patterns based on district characteristics

(district type, fiscal health, Basic Aid status, level of urbanicity and enrollment) or student characteristics (such as student performance, income, and EL status)?

– **Key findings.** Districts receiving relatively more Tier 3 revenue per pupil include high school districts and large urban districts, districts with lower-performing and higher-poverty students, and those with more English learners. There was substantial overlap between the types of districts that received more Tier 3 funds and more stimulus funds.

• **Distribution of Revenue Shares.** Which districts have the most Tier 3 and other restricted revenue as a share of all revenues? Are there identifiable patterns based on district or student characteristics?

– **Key findings.** For the most part, Tier 3 shares are pretty even across all districts, with only slightly higher shares in districts with higher Tier 3 revenues (high school, large urban, lower-performing, higher-poverty), but patterns are not as strong as those for revenue levels, and the correlation with poverty and performance go away when LAUSD is excluded. Before flexibility, larger shares of restricted revenue (overall) were found in large urban districts and in lower-performing, higher-poverty, and more-EL districts. After flexibility, these districts still have more restricted revenue, but the differences shrank.

• **Distribution of Revenue Changes.** Which districts have experienced the largest changes in Tier 3 and overall revenue per pupil (in dollars per pupil and as a percentage of all revenue)? Are there identifiable patterns based on district or student characteristics?

– **Key findings.** In dollars, the biggest drops in Tier 3 revenue per pupil were generally for districts with the most Tier 3 revenue to begin with (high schools; large urban schools; low-performing, high-poverty, and more-EL schools), but the results for size, poverty, and English learners are driven by Los Angeles. In percentage terms, there is no clear pattern. Districts in the middle of the distribution of student performance and poverty experienced the largest percentage drops in Tier 3. The reductions in total revenue per pupil also show no clear pattern. With the exception of Basic Aid districts, the percentage drop between 2007–08 and 2009–10 is similar across most districts, and districts with more Tier 3 revenue per pupil experienced somewhat *smaller* overall reductions in total revenue per pupil than other districts.

• **Spending Priorities.** How do districts spend Tier 3 dollars? How do they spend total overall revenue?

– **Key findings.** The majority of Tier 3 funds are spent on direct instruction, with a slight shift toward personnel over other items after flexibility. Tier 3 funding is largely used for general K–12 education; there was some increase in the share spent on alternative and adult education in 2008–09, but the overall levels are still small. Overall, the majority of total district funding is also spent on direct instruction and general K–12 education. The changes in expenditure shares over time are not large but districts do appear to have protected instructional personnel, pupil services, and district administration at the expense of instructional and instruction-related materials. They also protected pre-kindergarten and special education over alternative and adult education.

• **Spending Distribution**. Do districts with larger shares of Tier 3 funding have different spending patterns, particularly for instruction and teaching staff, compared with those with less Tier 3 funding?

- **Key findings.** Districts with more Tier 3 revenue spent relatively more of their Tier 3 funds on instructional personnel and "all other" functions (which includes maintenance and community services) and relatively less on other instruction items such as books and materials. They also spent relatively more of their Tier 3 funds on alternative education, adult education, and noninstructional goals, and relatively less on general K–12 education. However, districts with more Tier 3 revenue spent relatively less of their *overall* budgets on instructional personnel. Instead, relatively more of their total budget went to pupil services and "all other" functions, compared to districts with less Tier 3 funding. As budgets have shrunk, all districts have protected instructional personnel, special education, and pre-kindergarten, but districts with more Tier 3 revenue per pupil appear to be somewhat more aggressive about maintaining special education and reducing adult education.

We should keep in mind several important caveats. First, the SACS data are only available through 2009–10, the first full year of Tier 3 flexibility. It is perhaps unreasonable to expect to see dramatic changes in district spending over such a short period of time. I intend to update the analysis here as the data become available in the future. Second, the goal, object, and function codes used here for expenditures provide limited information about programmatic changes that districts might be making. For example, as long as funds are being used for instructional personnel, the SACS data cannot identify if those personnel funds are being moved from GATE or art programs to other subjects.[1] Third, because flexibility went into effect at the same time as major cuts in funding levels, it is nearly impossible to separate the impact of increased flexibility from the reduction in resources. It would be unwise to extrapolate from the patterns here into a future with additional flexibility but also increased funding.

Finally, districts may be reluctant to make any significant changes when there is uncertainty about the future of the flexibility provisions. Over the past three decades, there have been periodic attempts to reduce, consolidate, and streamline California's categorical aid system. On the one hand, the Tier 3 flexibility provisions could be seen as the latest in this history of reforms. On the other hand, when Tier 3 flexibility was granted in 2008, it was part of a larger budget deal that included significant cuts in the levels of funding, and few saw the changes as a deliberate attempt to truly "reform" the system (Fuller et al., 2011). The provisions are currently scheduled to sunset in a few years, and it is unclear whether all of the previous restrictions will be entirely reinstated. Governor Brown's proposal for a weighted funding formula would give districts even more flexibility, but (a) the time period analyzed here was well before Brown's proposal and (b) the success of that proposal is far from assured. For some districts, the possibility that the categorical program restrictions will be eventually reinstated certainly may affect how they use their Tier 3 funds in the interim. It may be quite a while before we have a clear idea of the real impact of giving districts freedom over this portion of their budgets.

---

[1]   Some of those personnel changes may be identified with the PAIF, collected as part of CBEDS. However, staff assignment information (indicating exactly what subject a teacher was assigned to teach) was not collected in 2009–10.

References

California Department of Education. Memo: Fiscal Issues Relating to Budget Reductions and Flexibility Provisions. April 17, 2009. As of May 7, 2012:
http://www.cde.ca.gov/fg/ac/co/documents/sbx34budgetflex.doc

———. *Report to the Legislature, Legislative Analyst's Office, and the Governor: Report on Expenditure of Funds Subject to the Flexibility Provisions of SBX3 4 2009–10.* July 2011a.

———. *California School Accounting Manual.* September 2011b. As of April 26, 2012:
http://www.cde.ca.gov/fg/ac/sa/

CDE—*See* California Department of Education.

Fuller, B., J. Marsh, B. Stecher, and T. Timar. *Deregulating School Aid in California: How 10 Districts Responded to Fiscal Flexibility, 2009–2010.* Santa Monica and Stanford, Calif.: RAND Corporation and PACE, 2011. As of April 26, 2012:
http://www.rand.org/pubs/reprints/RP1426.html

Imazeki, J. *School Funding Formulas: What Works and What Doesn't? Lessons for California.* Report for the Senate Office of Research, 2007. As of April 26, 2012:
http://www.csus.edu/calst/government_affairs/reports/School_Funding_Formulas_Final.pdf

———. *Deregulation of School Aid in California: Revenues and Expenditures in the First Year of Categorical Flexibility.* Santa Monica and Stanford, Calif.: RAND Corporation and PACE, 2011. As of May 4, 2012:
http://www.stanford.edu/group/pace/cgi-bin/wordpress/
deregulation-of-school-aid-in-california-revenues-and-expenditure-in-the-first-year-of-categorical-flexibility

Legislative Analyst's Office. *Reform of Categorical Education Programs: Principles and Recommendations.* Sacramento, Calif.: Office of the Legislative Analyst, 1993. As of April 26, 2012:
http://www.lao.ca.gov/laoapp/pubdetails.aspx?id=218

Loeb, S., J. Grissom, and K. Strunk. *District Dollars: Painting a Picture of Revenues and Expenditures in California's School Districts.* Stanford, Calif.: Stanford University, Getting Down to Facts Project, 2007.

Perry, M., I. Oregon, T. Williams, R. Miyashiro, J. Kubinec, L. Groff, P. Wong, and R. Bennett. *School District Financial Management: Personnel Policies, and Practices.* Stanford, Calif.: Stanford University, Getting Down to Facts Project, 2007.

Stecher, B. M., B. Fuller, T. Timar, and J. A. Marsh. *Deregulating School Aid in California: How Districts Responded to Flexibility in Tier 3 Categorical Funds in 2010–2011.* Santa Monica, Calif.: RAND Corporation, TR-1229-WFHF/DCKF/STF, 2012.

Timar, T. *Financing K–12 Education in California: A System Overview.* Stanford, Calif.: Stanford University, Getting Down to Facts Project, 2007.

Weston, M. *California's New School Funding Flexibility.* San Francisco, Calif.: Public Policy Institute of California, 2011. As of April 26, 2012:
http://www.ppic.org/content/pubs/report/R_511MWR.pdf